Intermediate Polyamory

Intermediate Polyamory

Poems by

Peter Waldor

© 2025 Peter Waldor. All rights reserved.
This material may not be reproduced in any form, published,
reprinted, recorded, performed, broadcast,
rewritten or redistributed without
the explicit permission of Peter Waldor.
All such actions are strictly prohibited by law.

Cover design by Shay Culligan
Cover image by Tanya Prodaan on Unsplash
Author photo by Gabriel Waldor

ISBN: 978-1-63980-821-2

Kelsay Books
502 South 1040 East, A-119
American Fork, Utah 84003
Kelsaybooks.com

for T & S

Other Books by Peter Waldor

Door to a Noisy Room
The Wilderness Poetry of Wu Xing
Who Touches Everything
The Unattended Harp
State of the Union
Gate Posts with No Gate
Nice Dumpling
Owl Gulch Elegies
Unmade Friend
Something About the Way
The Way 2
Midwife vs Obstetrician
Hats Off
Seven Quilts (essays)
Snowy Saplings
Understandings and Misunderstandings
At the Next Table
Time Can't Tell It's Being Told
Beginning Polyamory
Fairy Slippers
wellwhadayasay?
Turnstiles
14 Meditation Prompts and a Treatise on Noble Silence
The Third Way
You Alone Know
Tapadawhirld
Immigration Is the Essence of Democracy
The Way Fourth
One Can NEVER Predict the Past

Contents

First Date	13
Clit Size	14
Five Fingers	15
When Asked, During a Break, What Kind of Work I Do	17
Bad Mouth	19
How True	20
Frightened	22
Dancing	23
Anger or Rage	25
Aggressive	26
Radical Equality	27
First Date	28
Canyoneering	29
A Male's Notions About the *Male Gaze*	30
Two Urinations	31

X

Don't shrink from	35

X

Our Other Lovers	45
Night Moves	46
Pile Up	47
For the Pleasure of the Sub	48
Grand Finale	50
Poly or ENM?	51
What Is Love Anyway?	53
Love	54

X

One can only be tied up   57

X

Four Beauties   67
How Talk Works   68
Four times   70
Woman and Man   71
Gently   72
Proportions   73
Heterosexual Encounter   74
Spring and All   75
Pegged   76
No Pronouns   78
Professional Advice   79
Jealousy   80
Names   81
Two Rights   82
Ethics   83
Did I Change the Subject?   84
Sex Is About Talking Even More Than Touch   85
Blessed Shoes   86
The Empire Strips Back   89
Pubic Trim   91

First Date

A sparkling bar with the busy
sounds of many intimacies at once,
the bar slab itself a waxed slice
of a giant tree, dumplings shaped
like shiva lingams, and stems
of wineglasses thin as the blades
of young grass, and in the noise,
in answer to my question, I thought
you said *erotic peeing* and I
vaguely didn't want to know
anymore than that but later,
after we separated, I realized
you had said *erotic pain,* a subject
I would have been interested in.
I don't believe there was any
pain at all when we kissed.
Who knows what we'll explore next.

Clit Size

Was it with pride but also a small amount
of defensiveness when you described
your clit as the biggest clit you have ever
seen or heard about? We were in a snowy
forest talking and I assured you how amazing
your anatomy sounded but I also claimed
my partner's clit must be at least equal
in size. And later, when we were all in the
forest of the bedroom and I saw and touched
how your clit rose and rose out of your
beautiful and perfectly proportioned
frame I knew you were not exaggerating
and I saw how much pleasure it gave you
to be touched, when you were in my mouth,
hard and moaning. Perhaps size does
matter with the clit, even though it
does not with the penis.

Five Fingers

It was with great fear and trepidation,
that, after I placed one finger in your
yoni, I, at your gentle but insistent
instructions, placed a second, then
a third, then a fourth, inside you,
and though my partner, whose fist
is a little smaller than mine and who
had some experience, offered and
you expressed interest, in her fist
going all the way in, it didn't happen
that afternoon, and I was relieved
and disappointed. Afterwards
when all of us happily, quietly
lounged on the giant bed, and I
dreamed of walking alone in a
dark forest, my partner gently
mopped up the semen your
partner left on your slender
stomach, carefully folding the
towel on itself to find fresh surfaces
because there was a lot to mop up.
Her hands were against that
sticky moisture, something that
would have horrified me any
night before, but that day I
simply found it touching. Your
partner withdrew at the last
moment because better not
to have jizz in you for some reason

while you are in the midst
of chemo. I was looking away
at the moment of temporary
release and I regret I didn't see it,
magnificent as I'm sure it was.
And then, afterwards, I remembered
I had cum in your mouth
and wondered if that
wasn't a medical risk?
But you did say, on our earlier
snowy forest walk, something
about the acids in the cauldron
of the stomach destroying all
that enters. Before care, after-
care, and care during the act,
or the many little acts. Though
a fist entering will have to
wait for another day.

When Asked, During a Break, What Kind of Work I Do

I am not a watcher and I was sure
I would have a heart attack if I
saw what I saw—your big cock
in my partner's mouth, both of you
moaning with pleasure,
your Jack Lalanne body in full display.
And when we were all lazily
chatting afterwards, you asked
about my work, something people
are afraid to do, since I am in
the insurance business and they
are afraid they'd be bored or
worse, I'd try to sell to them,
but you asked with real interest.
Usually if people ask I tell them
how two mafiosos (one Italian, one Jewish)
threatened to kill me, and the
blackmail I still resist,
and the one bribe I gave (technically legal),
and the kickback I was asked for
and didn't give. Impressive
answer, I thought. But when
you asked, in your kind way,
though the other answers were
true, I answered more meaningfully
for you, how I spent most of
my days acting as surety,

for thirty years, so that if people
building neighborhoods failed to
complete the job, we would step
in and finish the roads, walks,
and sewers. Not as exciting
an answer, but more truthful,
for you who opened my eyes.
I hope someday I don't stop
sleeping if I start imagining
my partner leaving me for you.
Now I'm just happy to see the two
of you give each other pleasure,
even the hard from-behind variety,
something that makes me laugh
when I try it. For now, I dream
of all those new neighborhoods
I provided surety for,
and the cock sucking and clit licking
inevitably unfolding in them.

Bad Mouth

When I badmouthed my one
true love to my date, telling
her how my love told me
I wasn't forceful enough
when I kissed, and then we,
that is my date and I, kissed,
she quickly agreed,
yes, not forceful enough,
and so I kissed her with more
force and she said now
that's better. I never would
have changed my style
had she not agreed with
my love because I never
dare listen to her,
I love her so.

How True

Uncanny,
isn't it,
that the ad is
always for just
what we want.
Today's billboard
says *Nothing more
selfish than giving
another pleasure*,
with a beautiful
young person in
a tight tapering
pair of jeans.
A pair means
one article of
jean with two
legs, unlike a pair
of socks or gloves,
and more like
handcuffs.
The pair on the
billboard tightened
like a tourniquet
at the ankles
and I wondered
how the model
could ever get
them off without
scissors and if

there was a threat
to circulation.
The picture was
mildly pornographic
as a result of a skimpy
shirt above the
low-waisted pants.
I'm sure the model
was Actaeon, and Diana
was in the sfumato
distance. It took me
sixty years to notice
the difference
between jeans
and crave the tight
tapering variety
and I was so deeply
moved by the scene
that I didn't dwell
on the deep wisdom
of the caption, but now,
away from it all,
I can marvel at
how true it is.
Nothing more selfish
than giving another
pleasure.

Frightened

I thought we were smitten on our first date
and then even before I asked for consent
for a kiss you said you weren't feeling
like kissing but on our second date, without
asking, you leaned in and bit me hard,
several times, perhaps that was why
you didn't want to kiss on the first date,
you knew you were a biter and didn't
want to frighten me so early in getting
to know one another, but I am, indeed
frightened.

Dancing

You were dancing in my socks
and I imagine the lines in the air
they and your feet created,
the lines of Kubla Khan,
after the pen ran out of ink
but kept sliding across the page;
that's where wisdom is, in lines
disappearing as they are written.
It's not harsh at all to say I can
never be your lover because
I can't dance. It's not harsh
at all to tell me you're not
sure whether you want
to see me again. It is harsh that
the venue had to close,
early in the morning,
so you had to stop dancing.
Stop is the wrong word. *Pause.*
Now that we're separated.
I imagine you back in your place,
too excited to sleep, cleaning
your flogger, though it's best
cleaned by flogging. Patiently
brushing it, oiling with olive oil
and hanging it on the line,
next to the drying osha and
lemon balm. I don't know if I ever
want or wanted you to flog me.
And if we never see each other

again I regret I never showed you
my painting of The Marriage
of Heaven and Hell. It's only a
reproduction, but imagine that,
The Marriage of Heaven and Hell!

Anger or Rage

I am told anger, or rage, is the only
emotion men can safely express,
in our culture, and when my love,
dancing with another, started
to embrace and fondle the other,
watching, I became enraged,
and when the other saw my
anger, she offered to rescue
my love from me, even to drive
her halfway across the country
so she could escape me. I wonder,
did my love decline such a
generous offer because she is
too subjugated by the patriarchy
to accept? She probably said to
herself she has seen me cry when
looking at wildflowers. No excuse.

Aggressive

How many times have
I heard someone say
aggressive is not the right
word that I'm not enough
of, but everyone who says
it says they can't think
of the right word. They
don't want to use that word
but they use it, saying they
don't want to use it and
can't think of a better word.

Radical Equality

The last six women I met told me
they wanted to be dominated,
all variations on the theme
of having to run everything
in their lives—work, family, home,
and wanting for once just to
lay there and take in the pleasure.
Every time I asked what does it mean
to be dominated. I never learned
my lesson to ask only innocuous
questions. So I ended up never
hearing from them again after
I paid for dinner, the worst
domination of all. My worn
speech about radical equality
stayed folded in my pocket,
each fold part of a bow
that has never been untied.

First Date

On a first date she asked me
to tie her up, and I am eager to do it,
as long as she is patient enough to
teach me the knots, and I have
decided to keep to myself that
I am worried, due to the extremity
of our pleasure, I will have a
heart attack, and she will be stuck,
tied up in the remote bungalow
we chose, deep in the wilderness,
where no one will happen upon us,
one dead, one alive, for how long?

Canyoneering

When I plotted with you, my
longtime climbing partner,
to take my longtime love
canyoneering in Utah,
just the two of you, after I told
you my love and I were
free lovers, lovers with few rules,
you then pointed out, good
naturedly, that there
would just be wilderness
adventure and no lovemaking,
making an excuse, that your
lover would be jealous,
and I was, relieved, to
hear you say it, and my love,
later, was offended, that you'd
presume she'd be with you just
because she's a free lover,
especially since you'd never met.

A Male's Notions About the *Male Gaze*

I turn back three times like
an anti-hero in a Greek or Jewish
myth, to see her, but by then
the object of my gaze has woven
into the opacity of other futures.
Not looking ahead, I just miss
a light pole and ascribe the
almost accident to punishment
for my depravity and then I am
looking ahead again, worrying
about who saw me turn,
and why I am the only one
to do so, and if I wasn't so full
of desire would I turn just
for beauty?

Two Urinations

A man urinates inside a stall,
a giant rushing river, intermittent
though. I'm in the next stall,
grateful for indoor plumbing,
my own little stream also
intermittent. I imagine we listen,
intently, to each other's music.
I hope he's not one of my lover's
other lovers. Or, I hope he is
with her and he also smells
good and has mastered that
subtle and forceful rocking
motion.

X

Don't shrink from each's other

The tongue is at its best when it's barely showing—
A novice actor peeking out too far past the curtain

Be briefly gorgeous

Be embarrassed about being embarrassed, nothing more

May many people think you are their best friend

Never brag that your father met Marilyn Monroe

A pleasure to see someone we love stretch and yawn
And a displeasure to see someone we loath do the same

A queen should always be a drag

No instinct more tepid than heterosexuality

Overdo it. You can't do it over

There is no such thing as a good kisser

Shahrazad improvised

Touch with the toes

Entering and being entered. Concavity and convexity

Ideally, familiarity breeds unfamiliarity

The good quickie is full of slowness

If you like one out of three vibrators you're doing well

Don't touch me to make me hard, make me hard then touch me

Dance with abandon. Dance with abandonment

May everyone in the world be tramp stamped

Whistle a sweet song when you wash your lover's other lover's saliva out of their underwear

X

Our Other Lovers

Our other lovers are sleeping
in the other room. Naturally,
I'm the only one awake,
my curse and my blessing,
and I want to prod you awake
to make love, but I know
our other lovers will wake
soon and want me to join
them while you work for the
morning doing midwifery paperwork,
so I don't know what to do.
May everyone have problems like mine.

Night Moves

Feeling along your dark wall,
my palm brushes against the
painting of a fiery planet;
the painting, which I never
touched before, is soft and
sticky and yields like a wet
sponge, as if its oils were
still drying and the artist
had just stepped back to see
if there was anything else
to be done. And then my palm
was sliding along the firm
dark wall again; that's the
only way I know I'm not going
to fall down the stairs.
And now that other semen
and yoni juices and sweat
and perfume have entered
your bed with us, and I finally
return from my walk,
I take off my street clothes
and put back on my night clothes
to get back into bed next to you.
I had always rudely ignored
your complaints about entering
your bed with street clothes on.
Absurd request, I thought to
myself. How absurd I did not
always honor that request.

Pile Up

If we hadn't been with a pile of others
the last couple of days, I couldn't yell
you're a fucking tease when you got
up to go to the bathroom. I could never
have been that bold. And when you
came back I couldn't have whispered
in wildly inappropriate hierarchic
language that I love you most of all.

For the Pleasure of the Sub

Hard to believe in this city
of everything there is no shop
that just sells aprons. My love
and I are wandering around looking
as she is attending a tea later
as a Sub and wants to find not just
an apron, but the right apron
to wear with nothing else.
She will describe herself as
slutty, bratty, and flirty on a small
placard which will also indicate
she's ready for anything but may
change her mind. And shouldn't
that be the cornerstone of a
new religion—*I'm ready for
anything but may change my mind*?
She also wore a green tag for
further symbolism and I was
supposed to go as her Dom
and have a red tag but I'm
backing out and going to the
movies instead and then I'll
wait anxiously for the stories.
Aprons are perfect with their
suggestion of work and if worn
with nothing else they give a nearly
unobstructed view of the back-
side and partially obstructed
view of the front. Her basic

idea was something elegant
between a French maid's silk
and lace and torn-up linen worn
by a line chef at the local burger
joint. She is going to volunteer
as a Sub and believe it or not
volunteer Doms usually out-
number Subs two to one.
I love wandering the city with
her looking for the right apron
and if we get desperate we can
always go to our favorite sushi
bar where they know our names,
and ask to borrow an extra
apron for the night and they
won't be able to say *no*.

Grand Finale

Walking past saplings buried in snow,
just about to free themselves, thinking
of how, when you were out, to ecstatic
play all night and returned early in the morning
and seduced me, I thought it was a pity fuck.
I didn't realize it was a grand finale,
fucking the one you love last of all,
and instead of moping around all night,
I should have been sweeping, polishing,
buying flowers, dabbing my testicles
with citrus scent, showering, shaving,
and ironing my good shirt to make
everything as it should be for the grand finale,
sparkling, unless we simply fell asleep
in each other's arms, for it was four AM,
after all, and that's another kind of
grand finale, falling asleep together.

Poly or ENM?

That is the question my dear lover posed
to me after a weekend of beautiful talk,
food, and lovemaking. She said she is only
interested in poly, or love, and was afraid
I was merely ENM, or looking for sex,
and my answer was artfully evasive,
for whatever I wanted I knew I wanted her.
And yesterday, you, my partner, said your
therapist asked you what happens if one
of us falls in love and your answer was
we have no boundaries and all relationships
end in either death or separation, and that,
practically, we need to manage how much
time we give the other who we have fallen
in love with, so our partner does not get
too lonely and alienated, and we had a
nice polite talk about how much time
that would be and your conclusion was
no more than a few days a month
as I had suggested more than that.
Perhaps I then told you I could only
love you because I didn't want you to
love others. And perhaps you said
something similar to me for the same
reasons, though now you have forgotten
that declaration and are saying something
like you love everyone in the world
and what is love anyway. When I told
my therapist what your therapist asked

she said therapists are often voyeurs
and ask some questions to satisfy their
own curiosity and not to help,
and that question about love may be
an instance of that, if ever so innocent.
What happens if one of us falls in love?
What happens if anyone in the universe
falls in love? Every bet in the universe is off.
That is the nature of love.

What Is Love Anyway?

If someone says *what is love anyway* and you are horrified, remember, at least, that you are only horrified because you have asked yourself the very same question and also suspected love does not exist, not in the way you dream of, which may be where the trouble began, the dream.

Love

Who doesn't have mixed feelings
when a stranger calls us *Love*.
Are they degrading the word?
Have they instantly seen through
to our lovely essence? Or do they
simply love the whole world
as we are taught as children
and in houses of worship?
How suspicious I was of the
woman who said *love would
you please hand me that fork*
which she couldn't reach,
in line at the canteen. But I
handed it to her, tines facing me,
and I never heard from
her again, she who loves me.

X

One can only be tied up for the first time once

Better the last kiss be memorable than the first

Sex is sometimes better than talking about sex

It's taken too long for us to realize it's better not to ask
is that a man or a woman

There is no satisfying antonym for the word variety
and so it is difficult to prove that though variety
may be the spice of life, its antonym is the spiciest of all

Be a perfectionist who doesn't worry about perfection

Push and you shall be pulled

If you held back with me so it would be easier to cum later
with someone else, please block my number

One is either attracted to or not attracted to
It's not like one is more attractive than another

De young are good at sleeping, de elderly are good at sex

Eventually you won't need to know the details

The pleasure of pleasure is often greater than the pleasure of pain

When two people pass one another and each turns back
to look at the other, one will always stop looking before the other

I would never say we're all walking clichés, but
I can easily say I am

One can have sex continuously and still be multifaceted

Don't marry anyone else until you marry yourself

Listen to your breath and your partner's breath
Two antique clocks in a quiet living room

Is it wrong to flex when a loved one touches you? No
Afterall, you don't have feathers so you can't preen

Nonmonogamy may not be the cure for the disease of monogamy

There is no such thing as kink

French vanilla is the newest kink
And vanilla is the kink of kinks

The one who raised the idea of restraints is
often the one who wants to be restrained,
but they may not realize it

Sex negativity—disliking when anyone else has sex

X

Four Beauties

Four beautiful wrinkled
blue-eyed women
share dinner with me.
I pay for all of us,
not because I am an
agent of the patriarchy
but 'cause my eyes are
brown, though one of
the blue-eyed beauties
has charitably called
my brown *green,*
as she has taken
a shine to me,
and green, it appears,
may even be better
than blue.

How Talk Works

If you're not living in a warzone,
famine, or authoritarian theocratic
fascist state, conversation with
a new lover may turn to subjects
that show how good one or the other
is at noticing things in the world;
for example, my date pointed out
Christmas light wires strung tightly
high up in a tree trunk and branches
and she remarked how that trussing
could hurt the tree and I praised
her keen observation and to prove
myself, after stroking the trunk
once, gently, said I think it's a
sycamore, and she asked how I
knew and I talked about the thin
flaking bark, the olive-ish splotchy
color and the elegant dividing
of the branches, and I was poised
to continue on about Apollo and
Daphne (even though that story
had a laurel and not a sycamore),
and the 1920s WPA project
planting sycamores on all the tree belts
of the northeastern United States
and the great cutting a few decades
later as the sycamore became known
as the *dirty* tree, but I was silent,
because my new friend told me

her mother was a pilot and one day,
landing, her wing clipped a sycamore
branch. I asked, lightly, if she got hurt,
and learned her mother died that
day in the crash. My date, a young
woman at the time, was waiting
for her mother to come home
and take her to work. That was
forty years ago, but it will always
be yesterday for her. And then
we talked of other things, especially
mushrooms, the great decomposers
of everything but memory. And when
we parted she off-handedly
told me anti-zionism is not
anti-semitism; gratuitous,
I thought, to say then, but I
didn't ask her if in her whole
long life she was against the
existence of any other country.
I was mainly sad for her loss
and dreaming of a forest full
of mushrooms I was getting
lost in. Though I love people
and am eager to know my
date, I wished then
I was in that forest and unsure
of the directions.

Four times

you asked me if my partner
wouldn't be too tired after her long flight
to meet with you and your partner,
at Elixir, for absinthes, and exchange
of stories and unspoken words and looks
about whether the four of us would
fit together as lovers. There wasn't
an iota of guilt in your questions,
it was all a deep sense of concern
for others, and politeness, which I
immediately responded to in you,
and speaking of politeness, we were
all polite during our four-way hug
on the sidewalk outside the bar,
and I felt there would at least be
some friendships in-store, and who
knows what else. You would say don't
ask, let's simply see what happens.

Woman and Man

You want me
to be the man
who makes
the plans.
I am that man,
I assure you,
but can you
tell me where
to meet
tonight.
Please.

Gently

How you told me I was a fool
and should be happy my partner
was away having fun with others.
You told me gently, so I didn't
feel like a fool, just an idiot,
and then you touched
my chin and cheek and ear
and temple, gently, with your
left hand, and I was happy,
and happy even that
I have a lot to learn.
Gently, but with confidence.

Proportions

There is no greater tonic for desire
than to have your lover sleep with others.
However, your lover may need to be
reminded that even the best medicine
can be harmful in extreme proportions.

Heterosexual Encounter

Some women help dab up the semen
mess and some women don't. I don't
know if helping or not has anything
to do with feminism. And I don't
know if I am a good feminist.
I suppose it's all in the degree of
help given and the spirit in which
it is given and taken. Laying still,
half-dead while being ministered
to with a steaming wash cloth is
not bad. Somehow I always make
a mess. At first it seems like nothing
and then it's everywhere, that's how
it is with ejaculate, through the ages.

Spring and All

Early spring, which a *half-empty*
bloke might call late winter,
and I see a snowshoe hare
with the barest flush of gray
starting to form on its fat
white flank. We, the hare and I,
look into each other's eyes,
as creatures do, and at the
same moment we think
of Mme. De Cleves, the brilliant
beauty, rouging her white cheeks
red in her boudoir, dreaming of
her kind, handsome husband,
a favorite of the king, who she
adores but does not love,
and trying, unsuccessfully,
not to dream of M. DeMours,
the most dashing and charming
man at court, who she does love,
and who loves her, and who,
she suspects, will reject the
Queen of England's secret
offer to be King of England,
so he can, at least, have a
few discreet words with
her at one of the Louvre's
private parties.

Pegged

I am afraid you think you went
too far when you told me
your partner asked you to cuddle
and you gleefully told him
you wanted to tear each other's
clothes off and wildly embrace.
You noticed my visible scowl
and said you thought you said
too much. I'm guessing you only
told me in the first place because
I have pegged you as the Sub
and your partner as the Dom,
so you're trying to prove me wrong,
partly out of pride and partly
because you know I only respect
radical equality with no power
imbalances. And I did indeed
scowl, how could I not, but I'd
rather die than have you repress
expressions of joy. Even though
I hate all of this, I loved hearing
of your joy, and perhaps
that is the first intermediate
step for me. So, whatever reason
you told me that story, keep telling
stories. And regarding that word
cuddle which you have
castigated me so many times for
using instead of saying *I want*

to tear your clothes off,
I am sure that's all your
partner wanted to do, cuddle,
gentle cuddler that he is.

No Pronouns

When I tell people that we are going
to the airport, I, of course, say *we're
going to the airport.* But once, when
I was telling another lover, I paused,
and fretted, and then, somehow
said *I am going to the airport,*
both not wanting to rub it in with
the other lover that I was with you
and feeling guilty that I said it that way.
When I told you, my partner, on the
way to the airport with me, your first
solution was I should say *going to
the airport* only, leaving the damn
pronouns out. And then you, wise
woman, said it's best to say *we*
when it's we and *I* when it's I.
You gave me that advice right after
you told your other lover *I was
going to the airport,* forgetting
the royal or the plebian *we.*
I did feel lonely when I overheard
you say that, even though I was
holding your hand.

Professional Advice

The experts all agree it's best,
when one absolutely feels compelled
to say something, that one shouldn't say
it at all, and four times I listened
to the good advice and said nothing,
but now on time number five,
when the subject came up,
I did indeed say I didn't believe
you when you told me you told
your lover you couldn't join
them because you were with your
sister even though you spent
the day mostly with me
because you were honoring my
request not to discuss my life
with your lover. You knew
that request simply related to my
intimate feelings. My thinking
is you told them that because one
doesn't want to discuss one's affairs
with one lover with another lover.
It's a buzzkill. A sister is better.
I'm happy I didn't bring it up the
first four times because my conclusion
then was I shouldn't therefore believe
a word you said about anything.
Now I think it was just a harmless
white lie in the service of love.
And I am proud to be your sister.

Jealousy

Your husband gone just over a month
and we are out skinny dipping.
I want to hold your beautiful blacksmith
body but I am shy. Your husband
theorized the depth of love corresponds
to the amount of jealousy you each felt
when the other was with another lover.
You loved him but didn't feel any jealousy
at all, so you faked it. Faking jealousy.
I never heard of that. I know my partner
feels no jealousy when I am with you.
Does she not love me? What do you
think of your husband's theory?
I'm sure he'd wish you all the pleasure
you can have now that he's gone.
Do you have time for me? I don't
know any nautical knots to tie you
down, but I can hold your red-hot iron
rose in my handmade tongs while
you bare down on it with your
handmade hammer. I can do that
all day, in any heat.

Names

How strange that when by chance
we met your old longtime
lover and his new lover in the
market neither of us mentioned
it afterwards, and how strange
you chose to include both of
our surnames in the introductions,
you who have only used first
names previously, and I didn't
overhear what the two of you
said because I felt like I had
to attend to a new lover
who we share who happened
to be in the same aisle.
I know this could be confusing
to others, the old and the new,
our new lover and his new lover.
He introduced her with only
her first name and you introduced
our new lover with only
her first name as well.

Two Rights

Of course you blew me because you like
to blow me, but I wonder if an iota of it
was you knew I was going on a hot date
in a bit and my old man's refractory
period would stretch well beyond the
drinks in a public place and the *let's decide
whether or not to go back to her place
or mine* time, so therefore I'd just be
inclined to part early and platonically.
I did appreciate it, the pleasure, of course,
and I could approach the big night freer
of the burdens of desire, albeit an iota
exhausted, but with enough curiosity
to sustain a couple hours of talk. I talk
too much so I said too much and I both
regretted and was relieved I confided
in my new friend about us, and she
said you would never stand for the two
of us being anything more than friends.
You'd say she's wrong, of course, right?
Right. Two rights make a wrong.

Ethics

Upon hearing your advice that only I can
decide what to do after telling you about a romantic
interest who is temporarily separated
from her lover but their agreement is no sex
with others during the separation, when I was
expecting (perhaps hoping) for you to say
it would be unethical to pursue the interest,
your words freed me to pursue her
with abandon or at least cautious abandon.
I'm not sure what to think of the ethics of
your advice and whether to thank you.

Did I Change the Subject?

I wonder if you hesitated
to tell me about your
new lover because of her
age and not simply
because she is a lover.
And the way you blamed
me for changing the subject
before you could tell me.
Did I really do that?

Sex Is About Talking Even More Than Touch

And so the three of you were sitting sated
against the headboard when you finally said it,
how your lover no longer whispers clever
terms of endearment before during and after,
and he admitted his wife overheard him once
and didn't like it and so he stopped but now
that he knows of your disappointment he at
least calls you Tea Cake, not so clever
perhaps, but at least a gesture, which makes
it a little easier when you part.

Blessed Shoes

When I told your new lover,
who was kind enough to
extend a hand of friendship
to me, that I was afraid,
threatened, by the love
budding between you two,
he filled an hour with
small talk and then paused,
put a big hand on my shoulder,
and said it was difficult but
he was going to be vulnerable
with me and then said he
was indeed falling in love
with you, and he paused again
and told me it's also important
to him that you and I have
a solid relationship,
perhaps to allay his own
fears that he would
otherwise get in too deep
with you and have trouble
with his beloved partner,
and perhaps to allay my fears.
And when I asked you
if you were in your lover's
shoes, and I said what I said
about being afraid, what would
you say to me? Your answer was
you would ask gentle probing

questions about my fears,
which I believe would have been
even crueler than your lover's
answer. My answer, had I been
in those blessed shoes, would
have simply been, I am sorry
you are afraid, I will back off
immediately. But you were
right to remind me: he didn't,
after all, use the word *love*
after that terribly long pause,
he simply said he *adored* you,
and he was falling into *folly*
with you. Falling and folly.
Falling and folly. I'll stick by
my translation of that curious
word. Someone more generous
than I could ask isn't love the
whole idea anyway?
And aren't I being unfair by
not blessing your new union?
Am I the cruel one for prodding
the two of you to now say,
between your embraces,
that you're *just friends?*
I can't seem to stop
wondering about it so now
I am travelling the world
to ask lovers far and wide

how they would respond
to my anxious declaration,
if they were in those blessed
shoes and heard *I am afraid
you two are falling in love.*
More to follow. Though a
mean part of me dreams
of leaving you, since my
presence in your life seems
to be/is a precondition
for his/your love.

The Empire Strips Back

How I loved your hearty laughter
but worried it erupted because
you were uncomfortable next to me.
Behind us, a preppy young couple,
the night before their wedding,
taking their entourage for a night
on the wild side, or so they thought,
to see The Empire Strips Back.
The stripping and the music was
all pretty tame. You told me you
could immediately feel how
uncomfortable I was. Has
anyone ever noticed me
so quickly? And you are
intrigued by me because
you can't have all of me and
don't want to have all of me,
but perplexed, as I am,
and there is no guide to the
perplexed, even though the book
by that name has been around
for a thousand years. What
happened in your life that makes
you want someone like me,
someone who has others,
someone you may never
have brunch with on Sunday?
Were we more relieved or
disappointed by the bad stripping?

Your laughter is my guide.
The young couple was
singled out by the emcee
who made fun of their preppiness,
normative gender and relationship.
I imagine they imagine they will
have all of each other always.
They seemed pleased to be
singled out in the big audience,
even to be made fun of, on the
night before the big day
and the big life.

Pubic Trim

How I trimmed my pubic hair
for you so you wouldn't gag on it
and then you wouldn't even
agree to see me. Let that be
my epitaph.

About the Author

Peter Waldor is the author of twenty-nine books of poetry, including *Who Touches Everything,* which won the National Jewish Book Award for poetry. He is also the author of a book of essays, *Seven Quilts*. His book *Gate Posts With No Gate* is a poetry-art collaboration with a group of visual artists. He was the 2014–2015 Poet Laureate of San Miguel County, Colorado. His poetry has appeared widely in magazines, including *Ploughshares, American Poetry Review, The Colorado Review, Fungi Magazine,* and *Mothering Magazine.* He lives in Ophir, Colorado.

www.ingramcontent.com/pod-product-compliance
Lightning Source LLC
Chambersburg PA
CBHW031201160426
43193CB00008B/461